Table of Contents

THE CHANGING OF THE WAYS – PART ONE	4
JUST A FEW WORDS	5
POETRY	7
THE LONELINESS OF NEARNESS	8
THE SKIN COLOUR WHITE	9
WHAT DOES THE POET THINK	10
INFLUENTIAL PEOPLE	11
ABSENCE	12
MUSIC IN THE AIR	13
TIME	14
GODS	16
GODS II	18
SACRIFICE	19
THE SORB HEARTLAND	20
TOMB OF LOVE	21
FOR JAMES	23
LIBERTY	24
IN MEMORY OF MUDDY WATERS	25
HANS Christian KIRSCH - Writer and teller of tales	26
FLIES	27
STONEHENGE	28
SUNFLOWERS	29
ON A DOWNTOWN STREET	30
THE WAITING ROOM	31
SHOPPING WITH A COVID MASK	32
COVID 19 CONTINUED	33
MEMORIES	34
MEALTIME	35
A SHORT REFLECTION ON GLOBAL WARMING	36
PASSING THROUGH THE PORTALS	38
MY MUSE	39
GEMA CONFERENCE BERLIN 2021	40
LOCKDOWN	41
DEAR UNCLE SAM	42
ENTROPY	44
VIRUS	45
NO VICTORS NOR VANQUISHED	46
THE DESTRUCTION OF A GERMAN FOREST	47

LIFELINE	48
CONDEMNED	50
THEY SAY ALL MEN ARE EQUAL	52
THIS WINDY AFTERNOON	53
AFTER LISTENING TO BILLIE HOLIDAY	54
THE AGE OF REASON	55
MY GUITAR, ME, AND COVID 19	56
THE INACTION	57
LEARNING FROM GLOBALIZATION	58
THE DEATH OF THE PROTEST FOLKSONG	60
TECHNOLOGICAL DEVELOPMENTS	62
WHERE THERE'S A WILL THERE'S A WAY	64
CONFUSION	66
SOLITUDE	67
YELLER MOON	68
CROSSING THROUGH THE LIVES	69
ON THE TRAIN	70
TO LOVE, TO BE LOVED, AND TO LIVE	71
I DON'T KNOW WHAT YOU'RE DOING HERE AT ALL	73
REFUGEE	74
THE CHANGING OF THE WAYS	75
FAGS – (Slang for cigarette in the UK)	76
GLEN HAVALEEK SINGLE MALT	77
GLEN HAVALEEK II	79

# The Changing of the ways – Part One

By John Kirkbride

JUST A FEW WORDS...

Youth has finally and completely deserted me, gone AWOL so to speak, and left behind a collection of happy, not so happy, and a few miserable memories to be disembowelled and the bits analysed at leisure. But not yet. I know I could have handled some things better, used more things to my advantage, or just ignored situations which turned into affairs which caused problems later. But living from day to day, which many musicians must do, precludes organisation and is the cause of a very interesting lifestyle, which may not suit everybody, but which I've been lucky enough to have enjoyed

Like most people, when I try to imagine the various directions, my life could have taken had I done this or made that choice or had injected more energy in promoting the things that I could do well; things would have been more than likely easier, but I can't imagine more happiness. I was probably programmed from conception to be an idle son-of-a-bitch, become a rambling song writing musician, and one who simply enjoyed wine, women, song, and good friendship. Especially if I'd written the song which attracted the women who brought the wine with them.

It's maybe a bit like breakfast being over. Well, brunch really. My tastes in music have widened, and I enjoy classic music as well as blues these days, and I do avoid the culinary delights of McDonalds and other fast food, enjoying cooking myself. I also love playing my old acoustic guitar every day and anywhere. and writing music, songs and poetry.

When I buy jeans these days, which isn't often. I buy a comfortable pair which allow the balls to hang where balls are supposed to hang. The turning world has slipped another ratchet tooth. Regrets there are. But there are dreams. It's always possible that regrets still outnumber them, but I'm always optimistic.

You can never imagine just WHAT lies around the corner. I'm writing this in the middle of a Covid 19 lockdown which may have improved my home life but stopped the concerts momentarily. I miss the concerts which sometimes involved quite a bit of whisky drinking with the audience, poetry reading interspersed with musical bullshit and some seriously good songs. I'm still writing good songs. Every day. When happy with most of them, but occasionally some of them are so pessimistic that I play a Leonard Cohen album afterwards to cheer myself up.

But sometimes the goings on in this world can make a person a bit pessimistic.
And the guitar playing is always a delight. If lockdown begins to get you, just learn to play the guitar. You can take it everywhere. Piano players don't have that luxury. It's been my companion for the greater part of my life and was not only the means of meeting lovely and interesting people but also to earn money on the streets while busking. I once slept on a bench in New York's central park and would surely have been beaten up or worse if I hadn't serenaded my assailants with a couple of good (and funny) songs. Guitar is a kind of passport wherever you go.

And that brings me to poetry. Poetry is a beautiful and great part of literature. It's honest. It reflects life. Both yours and mine. Our world. And that, together with love, music and maybe the guitar, is all you need

POETRY

Food for the soul of the average man
Not reserved for some literary elite
Poems tell stories which make the mind wander
like a cunningly fashioned secret plan
Not directly of course, perhaps just a bit offbeat
Moving in rhythms like far distant thunder
to where the miracle of word and verse began

They capture a moment, a picture, a thought
and can conjure up an abundance of these
Moments forgotten, some of years and years ago
once more to the consciousness are brought
from their banishment in mental deep freeze
or incomplete, half hidden in shadow
to the realisation it's a memory you'd sought

Life is a poem then, but we often ignore
the magic of our day to day existence
Moments of laughter, love, even hate
but if you write it down you'll see there's much more
Your hand can record happenings with a poetic insistence
but when time passes, it is often too late
There is magic that time and distance can obscure

THE LONELINESS OF NEARNESS

People can be so self-absorbed that
their eyes are too blind to see
the cage they've built around themselves
from which they can no longer flee
Frail love is easily broken
through this oblivious abuse
the light of love is squandered
Neglect can also be abuse.

The loneliness of nearness
the gulf that is between
grows imperceptibly wider
like overlooked gangrene
When the distance from intimacy grows
too wide a bridge to build
and the river flows too swiftly to swim
Then love is finally killed.

The loneliness of nearness
This malady of the soul
Unconsciously destroys just what it seeks.
Love's presence, which consoles
Stranded in solitary intimacy.
To each their private dream
Will leave them in the churning flood.
Two islands in the stream

THE SKIN COLOUR WHITE

The skin colour white
an impractical shade
which is certainly bound for extinction
so why do we believe
that a pasty face
lends us an air of distinction?

The hours that we squander
at beaches and pools
with the oils and the creams and the spray
belies our opinions
of those darker skinned minions
from Jamaica, Gabon and Bombay

To be of mixed race
is a wise compromise
Obviously the best of both worlds
We see that quite often
and us less and less
And they have the more beautiful girls

As the races become mixed
Which they're bound to, of course
at some point we'll meet in the middle
And just prior to that
(the shock will be severe)
the paleface will play second fiddle

But becoming extinct
could have benefits, such
as to be displayed everywhere in nice zoos
with perhaps public copulation
so our last generation
could not just multiply
but also amuse

WHAT DOES THE POET THINK

What does the poet think.
Or does he think at all.
With the rifles pointing at his chest
His back against the wall
The fear of pain, the fear of death

The wrath at the unjust?
The fear that there is nothing more.
Than death, burial, dust
The love of verse, the inspiration
The hours spent in warm creation.
Can crumple, silent, to the ground.
Ungainly humiliation

What does the poet think?
As the soldiers take their aim
Do we see disbelief in his eyes?
Or acceptance of the blame
Or posthumous recognition
That's the least that he deserves.
In his still decomposition

At least his writings are preserved.
But, too late, the commander's shout
The triggers pulled; the shots ring out.
The poet dies, and falls, without

The chance to finish his thought.

INFLUENTIAL PEOPLE

I bought a TIME Magazine.
At the railway station Kiosk
And on leafing through it on the train
I noticed that.
Instead of current news
Its pages were filled with the lives and fortunes.
Of the world's one hundred
Most influential persons

I'd never heard of them.

Bart Simpson was not included.

Which would have been a great improvement

ABSENCE

Your absence is a rocking chair.
That calls me in my time of need.
To seek a crumb of comfort there
My thoughts and I are both agreed.

That absence is a hollow pain.
Which in this chair I can ignore.
The calm I seek returns again.
Provokes me gently to explore.

The warmth of memories we both share
Safe and sacred within me
Like familiar clothes that we both wear
Which guard our mutual liberty

Absence is a presence, then
Which disregards both place and time
And notwithstanding where or when
Reveals itself in words of rhyme

Our soul together is entwined
In trust close nurtured through the years
I may not be to trust inclined
But your absence does not awake my fears

MUSIC IN THE AIR

A saxophone's strong and confident voice
is a roller coaster complete with loops and rolls, twists and turns,
stomach churning manoeuvres accompanied by the screaming of
the terrified prisoners cum passengers inside/outside wetting their
pants and loving every minute of it
When played by someone like Lester Young, the Pres, who was
an ace, she became an extension of his body and was reminiscent
of a Spitfire fighter in full dogfight at ten thousand feet complete
with the roars and growls of the Merlin engine displaying its lack of
fear and the confidence that the assailant would be defeated.

The clarinet, on the other hand, has the aura.

of a lovely lady, a highly talented and capable soprano with long
sweet notes in her gliding voice. Like a sailplane riding on the wind
with lithe, flexible and artistic manoeuvres, delicately asserting her
dominance over the air.

And when she finally glides into land,

the rush of the wind over her wings is as the final prolonged note
of the orchestra as the symphony comes to an end. She rolls to a
halt, her wing dips in a curtsey, and the applause wells up in your
imagination.

The acoustic guitar quietly and confidently presents herself.
alone and unaccompanied.

Her six voices provide her with complete independence should
she so wish and supply all the lift and more she needs to keep her
dancing in the air. Like an ancient biplane doing what she was built
for, she is aware of the love and respect she earns, and she is
quietly confident that her wings will lift her over any musical
obstruction. Place a slide on your finger and she's a floatplane
gliding over a remote lake in some lonely northern landscape,
rising up into the air and into the blue.

She sings of freedom, and she allows you to sing with her.

TIME

Time passes in the one direction
I sometimes don't want it to go in
It's not that I want to be young again
but it's a fact that if I knew then

what I know now

things would have turned out differently

It's too repetitive

I'd like to turn the clock back and see
another dimension
Hear a ranting explosive torrential
monologue from Hitler
Put my finger up at the ten thousand simultaneous
Nazi salutes from the assembly
See the Spitfires and Hurricanes scramble, and
perhaps the charge of the Light Brigade

That might be exciting

See Jesus change water into wine and
sample the vintage
If it could compare with a good Bordeaux
or not
and if Nefretite was really as lovely
as the bust of her suggests

Have a quick look at Stonehenge
being built
That'd make your modern builder shut his mouth

See how every niche on the planet was peopled

See if Neanderthaler and modern humans got on together

Probably not, we don't get on together today. either
Strange extinct animals
A tyrannosaurus

Well , maybe not that last

Instead, time relentlessly and remorselessly moves in
the one direction
In which the atmosphere slowly gets more toxic
The inevitable next war, the atomic one, lies in waiting

We probably got this far
several times
In the history of mankind

but we didn't then possess the hardware

to make a decent job of it

GODS

Gods come and gods go
leaving their idols just about everywhere
Nobody even remembers their names any more
or if there was ever any need to know
Ancient civilizations, with love and with care
erected idols for the devout to tremble before
but the reverence somehow faded into disarray

We have a god who has lasted longer than most
A couple of thousand years or so
He faces competition, needless to say
but on a fair portion of the earth, he can boast
of faithful, of conquests, and he doesn't even have to show
his face to those who ask forgiveness on a
Sunday and then go home to drinks and Sunday roast

He'll be likely to continue for another millennium or more
He seems, until now, to be a just god, and fair
although in the past some disciples overdid the brutality
and were just as depraved as those others before
It seems to me that there's no way to justify, even with prayer even one religious fatality

But even today there are gods of great ruthlessness
who were doubtless present at the dawn of mankind
who invoke ethnic purity and what we loosely term nationality
to maintain dissidents in a state of toothlessness
but keep their followers united as in a single mind
in a movement which almost defies rationality
till you realise that the name of this god is wealth
who, together with his brother, power, enslaves the hearts
of those leaders to whom the needs of their respective nations
take second place to a certain stealth
Slowly, but surely, the leader starts

to summon power to protect himself, destroys reputations
of those who could be a potential danger to his life or health

There is one such god today who I need not name
The speed of his ascent was foreseeable, but still surprising
Confident, seemingly impatient, he has lost no time
in anchoring his church to sound foundations
and has shown promptness in dispensing blame
to those critics of his country's rising
The elected gods and leaders of rival nations.

and who has forced this lyric to have an acceleration in tempo:

Words of blasphemy from down
under proved to be a diplomatic blunder
The future of his creed to ensure
this god proclaimed that those with souls impure
should beget no children of their kind
and all critics their own business mind
but a lesser god was of another opinion
and not regarding his church as a lesser minion
declared this and incurred the wrath

GODS II

of the church of the mighty behemoth
who, with awareness of his empire's might
declared that he possessed the right
to sweep unbelievers from his land
and lesser gods could never understand
and he who such an opinion asserts
should be made to suffer where it hurts
Henceforth the god of wealth will cease to trade
until an apology is made

The lesser gods had never learned solidarity
to enable them to reply to such arrogant rhetoric
and most were fearful of seeming to criticize
such obviously inhuman barbarity
Still, the god of wealth gave a word of warning
which stifled any possible humane intentions
Morality has nothing if not variety
So forget the dream of a new day dawning
there is no sense in interventions
In this highly religious society

SACRIFICE

The most difficult thing about
committing a murder is the choice
of the venue beforehand

The spontaneous killing has no element
of beauty, generated as it is by a
rage exclusive to the human race, rarely
witnessed in the realms of the professional
carnivores, and with no forethought of how
to dispose of the remains after the act.

The art of the human sacrifice, so highly
developed as an element of religion in
previous advanced societies has been
neglected and sadly forgotten in ours.

Even the death penalty offers the victim
of the sacrifice no honour.

The Nazis, pilferers, not generators of
art
were unable to master the virtuosity
and flair of the human sacrifice throughout
their thirteen years in power although
they practised enough

and the contents of their primitive waste
disposal system has remained a part of
atmospheric contamination for seventy odd years.

THE SORB HEARTLAND

The dance of the dappling light
in the enduring silence
is not the only movement in
this ancient forest
She is waking to the annual ritual
of spring
for perhaps the thousandth time
Tiny buds of life appearing
New-born, high above
the covered head of the old woman
standing alone
Her prominent cheekbones betray
her Sorb ethnic roots
She is a survivor
The Nazis didn't quite manage
to annihilate all
She was little then
Now she is ancient
She has teardrops rolling down her cheeks
for those who will soon
be annihilated
Soon
the chain saws and the diggers
will arrive
firstly to murder the silence
that saturates this magic place
and then
to murder the trees
to mine coal
in the Sorb heartland

Hitler didn't manage to destroy
their bodies
But now, we will destroy
their soul

TOMB OF LOVE

You said that all the men you'd known
had worshipped you upon a throne
of love entwined with happiness and laughter
And then one day the crown you wore
had turned to thorns, and you were sure
his love was gone before, or was it after

You'd had a feeling all along
that much was right, but much was wrong
His flesh in yours was somehow less insistent
And when the flame of love had waned
somehow you'd lost but he had gained
The love which you had known had grown more distant

Your journeys through the world of men
had left you cynical, but then
you'd never sought a knight in shining armour
Then at some place I smiled at you
and having nothing else to do
you thought you'd entertain another charmer

We talked and loved and talked some more
and washed up on some fatal shore
after drifting in some warm caressing ocean
where lovers always seem to land
when there's no way they can understand
the stirring of an unforeseen emotion

We wandered on that lonely shore
You said that you'd been here before
A castaway just searching for salvation
Then came that harsh and bitter storm
that stole the heat within the warm
and froze you in your outcast isolation

You said that you were still afraid
that the storm which out of love was made
was waiting, and next time there's be no survival
So we both took shelter in the tomb
which offered hope within the gloom
and made love waiting for the storm's arrival

The storm is beating at the door
which we can't open any more
And somehow neither you nor I are trying
The tomb is sealed, I am the ghost
of one you thought you loved the most
and now we know that loving is like dying

FOR JAMES

It almost seems like yesterday
On Famagusta quay
The evening sun descended
and sank into the sea
And as the stars grew brighter
we couldn't sing another line
We sat there on the harbour wall
and finished off the wine

It almost seem like yesterday
But I know it's many years
since our souls were spliced and intertwined
as we talked about our fears
I listened to your story
and it was much the same as mine
as we sat there on the harbour wall
and finished off the wine

You left us a couple of years ago
after suffering much pain
and maybe I left it a bit too late
but Jim, here I am again
I sense that you can hear me now
It's as if I received a sign
I can still touch that old harbour wall
and still can taste the wine

LIBERTY

Liberty still does not yet invite me
to be her lover
after all these years of foolish worship

I am loath to choose instead
security
Daughter of governments
as a kind of capitulation

How could I ever forget
the incessant calling of my lady
Liberty
Who has often caressed me
and was gone when I awoke

Madam Security
If you demand that I choose you
perhaps I shall
but do not expect the obedience
of a faithful lover

for I will bring with me the memories
of the fiery forest
and in the cool of the evening
when your defences are lying low
I will place these memories between
your open thighs
that our children
may have the same choices

IN MEMORY OF MUDDY WATERS

He was born on a plantation, way down south at Rolling Fork
And the Stovall plantation was where young Muddy had to work
But he wasn't satisfied, he had a roving mind
He had to find the blues, and he just kept on trying

He taught himself the blues, blow the harp and play guitar
And in Clarksville in the 30's you could hear him play in every bar
But he still wasn't satisfied, had a roving mind
He just knew that he could make it if he just kept on trying

He cut his first recording in nineteen-forty-one
If you hear it now you know that a legend had begun
He was meant for something greater and kept on moving on down the line
He could never be satisfied, so he just kept on trying
He moved up to Chicago in nineteen-forty-three
Shouting I got the blues - hey blues take a look at me
He took the electric guitar and gave the blues a brand-new sound
And the blues of the Delta was no longer underground
So the blues went electric and Muddy was the wheel
He gave the whole world a music it could feel
The name of Muddy Waters became another word for the blues
Though he could never be satisfied there was no way he could lose

Well Muddy's left us now, but you still can hear him say
I gave the world the blues and it ain't never gonna go away
I made the blues a part of everyone and gave everyone a roving mind
So don't ever get too satisfied - but just keep on trying

HANS Christian KIRSCH - Writer and teller of tales

He was a travelling man
He was at home in many worlds and places
And the lives he wrote and read about
He could make you hear their thoughts and see their faces

When he was reading out loud
You closed your eyes to hear the music in his voice
It would envelop and hypnotize
It was useless to resist - there was no choice

We'd drive to gigs and yarn and play the blues
of Miles and Billie and Lester Young
Evenings his readings would take on the rhythm
It was almost as if his words were being sung

He's up there now with Woody Guthrie
Trading words with Ginsberg, Burroughs and Keruac
Would you believe, they're all on the same wavelength
It's Woody, Christian, Allan, Bill and Jack

Sometimes when I'm in concert
I can visualise the laughter in his face
So sometimes I pause and sing a song we sang together
A song he loved, Amazing Grace

FLIES

I cannot sit down mornings
and try to produce words
until I have disposed of
every fly in the room
including those of non buzz making
proportions

After this massacre is complete
I sit quietly for a few minutes
pretending to regain my composure
but secretly feeling the elation
of a job well done

When a faint buzzing noise
unleashes in me a few moments
of fanatical savagery

after which I stomp upstairs
and scrawl **SS** on each of my lapels

STONEHENGE

Suddenly they were there in the distance
Sticking up like the remains
of some long extinct bestial giant
Three free days and my friend's insistence
had urged me to take such pains
as to traverse this morass with legs uncompliant
and gaze at what I'd seen in books
Little pictures in contrastless black and white
Pages stuck together on library shelves
The things which the usual reader overlooks
But some who notice them think it might
be worthwhile to gaze upon these wonders themselves
I squelched towards them, cold, wet and alone
The April wind blustery in my ears
Lifted my eyes to gape in wonder
at these behemoths of unyielding stone
standing here for about five thousand years
Neither feeling the rain nor hearing the thunder
That must have been April of sixty-seven
Alone I was, no book of information
as to why it was here that was built this shrine
A tribute to determination, an incredible creation
but the stones were immute and gave no sign
And I'm here once again, fifty years have passed
Things have changed, now it's walled off with a fence
and the visitor centre charges eighteen pounds
Ah, the profit potential registered at last
But when I stop to think, it actually makes sense
The potential for graffiti here knows no bounds
Now it's summer and it doesn't seem so mysterious
Hordes of jeans clad tourists traipsing around
from China, Australia, Japan - oh, everywhere
Taking photos of each other, smiling serious
With the monoliths of stone rearing in the background
With neither love nor hate, boredom nor despair

SUNFLOWERS

It doesn't seem to surprise me
That I suddenly understand
the language of bees and caterpillars
as I walk beneath the sunflowers

Their golden heads
nod at me and silently command
but somehow seem to speak
and one sentence can last for hours

ON A DOWNTOWN STREET

On a downtown street all those years ago
I heard a negro play
The night was hot and petrified
and my life was changed that day
On a wooden crate he sat and swayed
and thumped his old guitar
With eyes wide shut he sang the blues
outside of some old bar

On a breathless night when I was young
I heard a negro moan
The words he sang were writhed in pain
and every word alone
The weary blues, for no-one there
were shimmering in the heat
while in the dirt he stomped his foot
to a personal secret beat

The blues, the beat, the night, the heat
electrified my soul
He sang the blues because it was
his subject, object, goal
He sang to the night as if it was
the vessel for his pain
And he could cork the vessel shut
before it hurt again

On a down town street all those years ago
a black man played the blues
In a threadbare jacket and worn out pants
No laces in his shoes
With simple words straight from his soul
he said what he had to say
He hypnotized, he paralyzed
He changed my life that day

THE WAITING ROOM

In the doctor's waiting room
The patients sit so silently
That you would never guess at all
That their hearts were beating violently

Are we positive or not?
Are we going to die?
The air pervaded with the silent sound
Of their inaudible plaintive cry

They're sitting there still wearing masks
So it's hard to read their faces
The fat woman wearing an ugly hat
And the fatter man wearing braces

Another old guy with his specs steamed up
So he sees even less
I imagine he doesn't want to see
It isn't hard to guess
Nurse pops her head through the doorway
Expectant faces turn
You can see their eyes shifting here and there
Feigning unconcern
"Mrs. Jones" says the girlish voice
And the room resubsides to gloom
The tension's high but you can understand
  It's deliverance or doom

The guy in the corner is staring into space
And you can guess just what he's thinking
What a ridiculous way to die
I'd rather die from drinking

The fat woman' d rather have a heart attack
Whilst in the garden, weeding
And specs steamed up dreams of a hero's death
Carried from the battlefield, bleeding
This Covid 19 has changed the world
But I know that some afflicted survive
But I don't think this lot has much chance
They all seem barely alive

It would be better if they all popped off now
Instead of occupying a hospital bed
You've had a good run, now your time is done
You're better off being dead

SHOPPING WITH A COVID MASK

Your glasses steam up and you can't see a thing
Not that there's much worth seeing
But just imagine the problems you'd have
if the buggers steam up when you're skiing
It's good that you'd have no clue to your fate
If you think it's just snow you don't worry
If you do see the tree then it's too bloody late
That'll teach you to be in a hurry

Covid masks cover your mouth and your nose
And at that they're very successful
The problem for me is when I've covered up those
Things begin to get stressful
My glasses steam up and I'm in a peasouper
Unfortunately without a white stick
I wouldn't describe it exactly as super-duper
With my arms waving I must look like a prick

Some say the trick is to remove the specs
But then you can't read the damn prices
Some people push their masks down to their necks
And other such inconsiderate vices
At the cash desk it's simply blind confusion
And it's surely the wrong change that you'll give her
So sod it I've finally come to the conclusion
Just phone and let the buggers deliver

COVID 19 CONTINUED

The lockdown seems now endless
but a thousand people have marched
through the city, packed together.
very few wearing masks, protesting
against their loss of freedom

They will, at least some of them will,
shortly learn what loss of freedom is
from a hospital bed plugged into an
oxygen pump

Its also my freedom these idiots
are stealing by promoting lockdown
after lockdown due to pure and simple

stupidity and selfishness

MEMORIES

You ask me why I do not grieve
For that which I did not achieve
In this turbulent life filled with many faces
Seasons, mountains, valleys, places
I've passed through and will not forget
the love, the hope, triumph, and yet
some faces linger more in mind
than others forced to leave behind
The welcoming hug, the tender smile
Places where I tarried awhile
There where once true love was shared
doors were opened, hearts were bared
Secret fears and longings spoken
And later, when some hearts were broken
Memories with some regret
At those, not forgotten and well met
A miscellany of memories I carry still
This treasure I bear and always will
  No, there is no place for sadness
When recalling these moments so rich in gladness

MEALTIME

We kids took it in turns
to eat our meals in the
kitchen
because the dining room table
was too small

I liked it when my turn came around

The absence of table manners was
without comment
and from my side
the absence of bland conversation
allowed me to concentrate on
getting my belly filled

And the burp at the end
was deeply satisfying

A SHORT REFLECTION ON GLOBAL WARMING

There's a growing awareness that global warming
has changed our lives in subtle ways
I've been told that this is just the beginning
Icebergs melting, no new ones forming
It's surely time for action, time to appraise
the consequences of mankind's thoughtless sinning
against nature, on which we all depend

We are children of nature; from thence we came
Stern warnings have often been given
to try to draw our attention to the climatic trend
Nevertheless, it took us fifty years to admit our blame
for the tunnel vision which has relentlessly driven
the earth, not as invulnerable as we would like to think
to our abuses, to reach almost the point of no return

The changes we have provoked cannot easily be undone
A thousand years in nature is a single blink
and mankind has always been reluctant to learn
from his persistent misdemeanours, but anyone
can easily realise that a league of nations linked
together in agreement to turn back the clock would earn
a collective sigh of relief from those future generations

relieved to be able to breathe clean and unpolluted air
and bathe in and eat the fish from clean unpolluted waters
Now must be the time to join hands in the joint creation
of a giant project supported by human beings everywhere
to save the earth and the future for our sons and our daughters

to continue.......

The above was written in 2007
and since then some changes have been made
Unfortunately the lobbyist's were in lobbyist heaven
and succeeded in getting things delayed
Fossil fuels will remain for at least thirty years
in spite of a heated debate

It didn't help much, just awakened my fears
that we're doing too little, too late
In spite of a widespread rejection of plastic bags
many end up in the sea

I realise that radical changes will always have snags
but some are a mystery to me
It might be better to teach ecology in schools
To start, if you like, with our youth
Then it won't be so easy to treat people like fools
Governments will be obliged to tell people the truth

PASSING THROUGH THE PORTALS

Passing through the portals
of the hospital
is like a foretaste of doom

Having ignored the necessity
for so long
it becomes a natural
part of your being
But when it begins
to dominate your daily life
Your actions
It's time to submit to

The knife
Which has always represented
Death

But the ones here are presumably
different
They're supposed to preserve

Life
But they probably look the same
as the others

But they probably
knock you out
before they put you down
So you won't
see them

anyway

MY MUSE

My muse just popped out
for a couple of bottles of red
and maybe a sixpack

He's been looking on in disbelief

at the time we've wasted trying
to write poetry

while longing for a drink

As the verse gets longer
The thirst gets stronger

GEMA CONFERENCE BERLIN 2021

We have drunk the wine of friendship
you and I
and later tasted the fruits
of love

A part of life's journey we travel led together
until the reluctant goodbye tears and kisses
forced upon us by life's circumstances

We were close, our love joyous
Tasting and sampling life and love together
gave it a flavour which has been stolen

And now. Some years have gone by. We meet again
at this conference

I may not embrace you
I cannot smile at you
or kiss you
or hold your hand

Not even shake your hand
We sit. Six feet. A thousand miles
separating us

wearing Covid masks, I cannot even mouth the
words I long to say to you

The pain
is devastating
I hope we are writing the same song together
in our bleeding hearts

LOCKDOWN

Freshly fallen and pristine snow
unblemished by footprint or treadmark
lies outside my window
The actual image. of a Christmas card
in the heart of the city is invariably
swiftly sullied by the first motor
vehicle, pedestrians walking their
dogs, and snowballing kids

But now it simply compounds the impression
of incarceration and isolation
in the heart of a city
partitioned by lockdown
Sunday. Shops are closed and there is
no other reason to disobey government
recommendations to remain at home.

So it appears that everyone is doing just that
A gloomy and dispiriting vision
A dead world totally devoid of life
No bird sings
They seem to be aware of the unusual
absence of mankind
with which they have shared this city
for thousands, if not millions
of sparrow generations
There are trees dividing the two lanes
of the road which passes beneath my
window, and the white translucence of
the snow
clinging to the bleakness of
their winter branches I have seen
somewhere before.
Then I know, in the paintings
of Bruegel
No, this is not a vision of Christmas
Rather it is a vision of capitulation
The obliteration of life
And if Covid 19 should succeed in this
would the sparrows return in the spring

and would they regret our passing

DEAR UNCLE SAM

The mistrust simmering beneath your confident facade
is clearly not just confined to you
It may possibly be due to some hitherto unknown genetic error
On the one hand, you supply aid, not just to your own back yard
but you also supply troops to assist in the rescue
of those who are victims of unholy terror
But on the other hand, you regard the minorities in your own country with contempt, even hate
and can offer no logical reason as to why
this is so. Convinced of our racial superiority
white people apparently possess the right to create

a society in which a black man, accosted by police, may die
You changed our culture. You gave us rock, jazz, blues
Presented to other countries a benevolent and generous face
Powerful, you were treated by others with respect
and if most people had the right a culture to choose
it would most certainly be yours. A democratic birthplace
which viewed from a distance appeared to be perfect
but cracks were appearing and filtering out
as many as fifty or sixty years ago

We read occasional articles about racism, Ku Klux Klan
and we began to wonder. A few seeds of doubt
were sown, but your glamorous profile still stole the show
Who thought, in the fifties and sixties, about rights of man?

Without you, an evil empire could not have been defeated
and here in Europe life would now be a living hell
Your strategic umbrella allowed us to enjoy the longest peace we'd ever known, and many years later the miracle was repeated when the wall dividing Europe finally fell

We saw atomic weapon proliferation finally cease
But the struggle is incessant, it will surely come again
that we see other nations girding as for war
The craving for power, the yearning for might
Yes, this human genetic error in the hearts of men
could force us to return to the place we were before
To sink once again into the darkest night

We have certainly offered too little by way of return
This peace, this good life, does not come for free
But we have all been guilty of turning a blind eye
Perhaps the time has come for mankind to start to learn
to open that blind eye so that we can finally- all see
And when that eye is opened then it will be time to ask why
The life that our fathers fought for cannot safely be kept
with any form of racial dissonance brewing in our hearts
Can it be so hard to see a neighbour as a friend?
of course, there was some awareness of this, but most slept
Mankind is one creature, but one of many parts

and when we have learned this, then hate may one day end

ENTROPY

The entropy of my life
can be easily observed
by the old and tattered clothing
and the dog eared and much read
books scattered everywhere in my room

Trips to the doc become more frequent
As do trips to the loo
One is still aware of breasts
but is also more aware of their
inaccessibility

And English sports cars
though desirable
are too near to the ground
to allow sprightly ingress and egress

The entropy of my life contains
the dust of half remembered
incidents and conversations
Kisses, but also anger
Some successes
but more defeats
The vague memory of
a great love that almost
broke my heart

Songs that revolutionised my thought
Now pallid, outdated, and meaningless

Strangely enough, great art such as that
of Beethoven and Mozart, Van Gogh and
Leonardo, Shakespeare to Tolkien
remain unaffected

VIRUS

The virus is our enemy, but can sometimes be a friend.

A virus stopped the first world war it brought it to an end.

NO VICTORS NOR VANQUISHED

Who will be the one to laugh the last
When this sad and tragic theatre is past
With many a tragic tale to tell
And many a rumour to dispel
About who got sick and who got well
And who looked on aghast

It came to destroy our flimsy nest
A challenge to mankind, a universal test
A call for each and everyone
To rise up against this invasion
Some disbelieved, but some looked on
And were shaken and distressed

There were others filled with defiant energy
Young, impatient, yearning to be free
Exulting the night with united sense
That youth was a bastion of self-defence
United in a naive pretence
That this could not happen to me

Our enemy, invisible to our sight
With arms against which our weapons were too slight
We were compelled to mask our fear
It travels through the atmosphere
We'll win this battle, don't interfere
Take refuge from the fight

There are no victors nor vanquished in this war
Who will be the next to pull the shorter straw?
Restraint is the key to disarm the threat
The days grow longer and we'll not forget
And let us hope that these memories will let
Us cherish love and life and understanding
a little more

THE DESTRUCTION OF A GERMAN FOREST

Ancient communities have been razed to the ground
And now it's the turn of the trees
Bulldozed, living, from the land
As if they were some disease
Some as old as the written word
So proud against the sky
If they could talk they would surely tell
The truth before they die

We know in our hearts that you no longer need
To burn that choking coal
Disfiguring land and ripping out
The urn of our father's soul
This once was the oldest forest we know
With nature so wild and so free
How can you lie with the promise you made
To alternative energy

In a year or two you will come to regret
The crime you're about to commit
Tearing out beauty and ravishing life
For an ugly soulless pit
You talk of pollution, the tainting of air
With not even a cynical laugh
But the ghosts of all life in the Hambacher Wald
Will bear the aftermath

LIFELINE

Rolling down your lifeline - hear the lonesome whistle blow
Heading for your deadline - got your ticket and you've got to go
Following the shoreline - see tall ships out at sea
Heading for the skyline - by immutable decree

Life moves on on an unseen track with a multicoloured trail behind
If you look to the front all you see is black,
it ain't good when you're travelling blind
Sometimes you're speeding on down the line, sometimes it's just a crawl
Somtimes you just have to sit and wait and nothing moves at all

Sometimes the tracks run parallel, and you get the chance to see
That you're not the only one who can't control his destiny
And then those tracks run into yours and you find a brand new lover
Sometimes you meet a long lost friend, a sister or a brother

You crash onto a mainline all at once, lit up as bright as day
And you seem to think you've got this chance to say what you need to say
But nobody here can hear a word as a whistle starts to blow
The fast express just moves on by, you're roving much too slow

Rolling down your lifeline - hear the lonesome whistle blow
Heading for your deadline - got your ticket and you've got to go
Following the shoreline - see tall ships out at sea
Heading for the skyline - by immutable decree

You're back on the branch line, red with rust, like blood beneath your wheels

Your fellow passengers are all gone, you know lonesome feels
And the trees thin out and you have no doubt that you're heading for the desert sand
And your hope grows thin and it chills your skin, you're headed for an unknown land

You suddenly sense that the end is near you can feel it up ahead
You think to yourself if that's all there is, you're better off being dead
Just a lean-to shack by the railroad track with a creaking windblown sign
But to your surprise you roll on by, keep moving on down the line

Strange creatures leer but you have no fear in this vast and barren land
But something tells you your destiny doesn't lie here in the sand
Somehow you're sure there's something more, there's something you're bound to find
when the eagle cries you'll realise the dream of all mankind
Rolling down your lifeline - hear the lonesome whistle blow
Heading for your deadline - got your ticket and you've got to go
Following the shoreline - see tall ships out at sea
Heading for the skyline - by immutable decree

CONDEMNED

At his final confession, the priest urged him to come to his senses and cleanse his soul before God, but the subsequent wild laughter of the condemned man terrified the clergyman and gave the cell something of the atmosphere of a lunatic asylum.

Nor was there anything the priest could say or do to quieten him. The result of his efforts terrified him even more as the prisoner, who was obviously completely

mad, grabbed his hands and danced his unwilling partner round the cell, knocking the table over in the process. Finally, exhausted but still chuckling to himself, he released the priest and leaned good humouredly against the wall.

''O father, I swear that that's the funniest thing I've heard since they put me in this miserable hutch. A man needs a laugh now and again and sure there's no time like the present in my predicament" He laughed loudly again, then sat down on the bed and was silent.

"Come now my boy. There's no call for this laughter and frivolity. There's absolutely no humour in this situation. None whatsoever" The priest spoke dogmatically as he warmed to his task, and leaned forward

earnestly in his chair. "There's many a man stuck on the battlefield who would be happy to make his confession, but you, my son, waltz around and laugh in the face of the Lord himself. Now, before it's too late make your confession and let's have no more of this foolishness"

The little speech brought a fresh bout of mirth from the prisoner, who nevertheless this time clutched his stomach in an effort to control himself. The priest, red faced and slightly angry, stood up and addressed

the spluttering sinner.

"This little joke has gone far enough. I can't understand what, in the name of the Lord, you are laughing at, but I can assure you that if you don't pull yourself together I shall leave this cell and you will receive no further help on this side of life" .

The condemned man quieted immediately, and cast his eyes downwards to meet those of the priest.

"Father, you must yourself most certainly see something of the stupidity of the situation. I've never been to church in my whole life, even though I was born a Catholic as you yourself know, and I've never been baptized. All my life I've been guilty of what this society calls

crimes, but to me were merely a means of survival because, I tell you straight, nobody gives you the time of day unless you take it for yourself. And now, for one of these so-called crimes I'm to be hanged". He shrugged his shoulders. ''I'm not about to say that the sentencing is unjust, but I'll l tell you this: If I should sit and relate all of my doings to you it would take until this time next week, in which case

you would have to accompany me into the next world, and if you tell me, as you do, that in the last moments of my life I will merit forgiveness by merely bragging about my exploits, well , I just don't believe it."

"May the Lord have mercy on your soul " breathed the priest.

The smile was still playing on his lips as they led him to the gallows.

THEY SAY ALL MEN ARE EQUAL

They say all men are equal, but some are more equal than others
Open your eyes and look at your so-called sisters and your brothers
And if your skin is different, when it comes to the bottom line
You're the one who'll take the rap when things ain't going fine
That's the pecking order, and that's just the way things are
It don't matter if you're in fine clothes, and driving a fancy car

Don't entertain illusions when you're with your fellow men
Basically things are just the same as things were way back then
You're gonna have to pay if you bite off more than you can chew
The white man does what he wants to do but remember you is you
That's the pecking order, and that's the way things have to be
And you know that that ain't logical , you're a citizen and you're free

Some things have gotten better, well at least they ain't got worse
But just one disagreement and things slide into reverse
When the cop comes round the corner it's at. you he'll point the gun
And he'll scream "come here nigger tl he won't whisper "take it easy chum"
That's the pecking order, and it ain't too 'bad to bear in mind
When things start getting stressful , even your buddies ain't too kind
When you're talking with the girlies just remember to keep your place
Why it ain't too many years since you've been part of the human race
The ladies may not give a shit, but it's the boys you have to watch
Beating up a black boy put's their egos up a notch
That's the pecking order, and you'd do well to. bear in mind
If you ignore unspoken rules they'll pay you back in kind

They say all men are equal, well so they are in many ways
But don't disregard the unspoken rule that no-one ever says
It pays to sit at the back of the bus though no-one says you should
And it pays to avoid the white girls, although you know you could
That's the pecking order, and you and I know that it ain't right
We ain't reached the age of equality, we're still heading for the light

THIS WINDY AFTERNOON

My sword turns to plasticine
on this windy afternoon behind
the typewriter, and while I prepare
to immortalise my irritation, I
cannot ignore the fact that this
morning I heard news of the forthcoming
marriage of my brother. He never
listened to my advice anyway. The
wind is rattling the window. I hear
the kettle boiling in the kitchen

Right. Tea's ready. Now, where was
When this damn wind stops I'll
write him a letter. I've never met
his girlfriend. I wonder whether she
smokes and likes kippers. Or caviar.
Does she buy flowered underwear from
Marks and Spencer. Does she shave
under her arms and are her teeth white
and all there.

My head is filled with thoughts of
this girl. Someone i've never known.
She'll marry my brother.

The tea's good.

AFTER LISTENING TO BILLIE HOLIDAY

Billie had blues in jazz
and she sang them both together in style
She can even today open up your heart
Force your tears but make you smile

She sang from the depths of her coloured soul
Just listen to that black girl moan
Then comes the answer from the one she loved
Lester's stalwart saxophone

You can hear where she's coming from
and it can cut you like a knife
Her little girl craving love and understanding
and the resignation which coloured a black girl 's life

Open your heart and mind to the young Billie
Your tears will fall as she sang before the end
Her surrender of her soul is impossible
for any white person in this world to comprehend

THE AGE OF REASON

My orbit passed the age of reason
but I was unaware
But now I know that even if I'd sensed the change
It would have seemed too strange
for me to care

I passed the age for laughing
Never laughed too much anyway
I felt no need for having fun
and though my life had just begun
a day was just a day

I passed the age for listening
to the advice people offered me
I only heard the things I thought
I'd need to plant the seed
of liberty

I passed the age of dreaming
Ignored my dreams and let them fade away
A dream's perfection in the night
grew paler in the morning light
Then faded where it lay
I passed the age for loving
Left love still veiled in mystery
Each life I shared would be the last
but when the joyous storm had passed
the wind would set me free
I passed the age of memories
Discarded those I thought I'd never need
The barren museums of my mind
were locked and shackled, speechless, blind
too cold, too shrivelled   to see

My orbit reached again the age of reason
My eyes had been opened, great vistas lay before
I stood high in a point in time
where memories shone like beckoning signs
Every one an open door

MY GUITAR, ME, AND COVID 19

The absence of concerts begins to take its toll
The voice of my guitar, and mine, are stilled
A life devoted to music and lyric was always my goal
Now the joy of song has been abruptly killed

I think about this pleasure I have shared with many friends
The joy of harmony moving in the air
You'd be forgiven for believing that such wonder never ends
This human need, remove it if you dare

The sadness lies in silence, the beauty of the word
That and music is the greatest gift of all
I found joy in all the symphonies and songs I ever heard
And words of wisdom in the songs that I recall

I look at my old guitar, that workhorse, leaning on the wall
She's silent, still , inactive, it's as if she sleeps
But I know that it's a lie, George Harrison said it all
While my guitar gently weeps

THE INACTION

The inaction begins to stifle the brain
This lockdown never ends
Look through the window, stare at the rain
Shall I go out? It depends
on if I need to go to the shops
for bread or milk or sugar

Or shall I wait till the downpour stops
Get out, you lazy bugger
Been sitting here all morning now
drinking endless cups of tea
considering between bouts of yawning, how
the rest of the day will be

Streets look empty, course they are
Nobody likes to get sodden
And my anorak smells a bit bizarre
If anyone notices, sod em

But how did it get to smell like this?
It's as if a cat pissed on it
And there's: nothing worse than feline piss
And it won't improve this sonnet

Maybe the rain will wash off the stink
You never know your luck
But it's now or never now, I think
I'l l go out now - oh fuck!
Broke a shoelace, just like that

and I haven't got another
I sometimes am a stupid twat
Some people would say mother...
Well , no need for that kind of language
I'll have to go, I've got no bread
Can't even make a sandwich

So I'll do it now, the streets are dead
There'll be nobody around to see
the dickhead with one shoe hanging off
and reeking of moggy pee
There's nothing in the fridge to scoff
and I'm getting an appetite
This rain will land me with a cold or cough
Life is full of shite

LEARNING FROM GLOBALIZATION

Amazing what you can buy in the shops these days
Summer produce in the middle of winter
An impossible dream when I was a kid

Globalization

I bought a box of cherry tomatoes
in my local market
I've always enjoyed eating them, but
these had a rare and wonderful texture
and were exceptionally sweet

Probably from some greenhouse in Holland
I thought, but on examining the label
I read
Produce of Senegal
Senegal , I knew nothing about it
I found it on the map
West Africa.

What kind of country was it?
I wondered
What kind of people lived there?
Black people obviously
Were they poor or did they have
a good standard of living?
Were they treated well by
their government?
Could they buy these tomatoes
too?
Now I know where Senegal is
The rest I'l l check on the
Internet

You can learn from globalization

CIGARETTE

How can we all get drunk tonight
without a cigarette
The world is getting crazy
but how crazy can it get
This bar should be filled with happiness
But I ain't seen none yet
How can we all get drunk tonight
without a cigarette
Standing in my local bar
on a nameless Saturday night
I stick a roll-up in my mouth
and turn round for a light
When a big guy grabs my arm
and almost makes me spill my beer
"Hey buddy, if you want to smoke that thing
get your arse rightouta here"
So I'm standing in the pouring rain
with about thirty other folks
Some with soggy cigarettes
and some with soggy tokes
It gets to raining cats and dogs
Can't get my smoke to light
Oh Jesus Christ almighty
what a shitty Saturday night
I could take two sixpacks home tonight
and drink them in my room
And smoke and drink till five o'clock
in a hazy foggy fume
With the New York Yankees on TV
I'll kick my wet shoes off
And puff right on till the morning sun
to feed my smoker's cough
How can a simple guy face the world
without a cigarette
I don't believe it I'll never achieve it
I wouldn't take a bet
It's the same the whole world over
Little freedoms are a crime
I'm just a layabout, so count me out
of this smokeless pantomime

THE DEATH OF THE PROTEST FOLKSONG

I am filled with deep sorrow, my good and great old friend

We are experiencing together your extended and certain demise after yours being for a century the voice of conscience in this western society. It's especially tragic that your end should come at a time when more people are beginning to realise that without your tireless influence in questioning our deference

to the powers that be, those faceless ones manipulating the system from behind, we would still be living in a class divided society such as that which was prevalent until not so very long ago when a particular accent or clothing could mean a banishment to serfdom or doors opening to higher places; a continual source of anxiety

for those striving to get on against the entrenched might of the status quo

Originally, yours was the voice of the street, people would stop and listen to what you were singing about, and when you eventually graduated to the pubs and clubs the audience was able to invest more time in digesting your message, and I myself have seen tears glisten

on the face of a woman listening to a song decrying war, punctuated with pauses to reinforce the words, not necessarily in words of rhyme, and it was a message initially coldly ignored in the political world, much less publicized in its rousing speeches, but one affecting lives in every level of society. Youth sent off to war, possibly to die for some cause generated by the failures of some diplomatic commission resulting in death and disablement, devastating families, parents, wives

all of whom were led to believe that war was necessary, but not told why

Wars have been terminated with the help of your message, brought tears to the eyes of those who took time to think about what you had to say and who acted on your words, a voice from the past coming from way back in Africa and hence to slavery in the cotton fields of the south. Fear of punishment led protests to be disguised as field hollers, all the slaves singing in traditional african harmonies, a concealed attack on the slave system, united with a sadness which later became the blues

The blues incorporated anger at the subservience of the black population of the USA, became widespread internationally after the abolition of slavery, was later adopted by white musicians and began to perfuse

popular music and thus to rock, not confined to any single nation but spread throughout the world, a great musical and cultural acquisition

But now, my friend, you face death. Your voice stilled by Covid 19 Clubs closed where once your voice was heard, pubs insolvent, street music, busking, strictly forbidden for fear of infection, the trash heard on radio or television is

as if you had never been

Musicians of my acquaintance have forsaken their involvement and are attempting to survive in a less valuable musical direction

The legacy of Guthrie, Seeger, Dylan, those who sang with your voice is long forgotten and is ancient and trivial history to the new generation which appears to be concerned purely with its own personal needs

Musical protest, a language with consequence, would not be their choice For a continuation of the movement there seems to be no veneration

Just a self-devoted personal longing to be seen, and to succeed

TECHNOLOGICAL DEVELOPMENTS

Technological developments
could assure our doom
or hopefully our salvation
either rendering the earth
a planetary tomb
or by stimulating creation

for mankind, an aggressive beast
has throughout his history never ceased
to employ his manipulative masterpiece

Nation versus nation

The threat of retaliation
could counteract a threat against stability
by a hostile power compelling us to overreact
to assess our military capability

As history has always shown
a defending nation, standing alone
in an illusion of peace, is always prone

to have little or no strategic ability

To underestimate the probability
of conflict
by military means
can be indicated by the tendency
to predict
dissengagement when diplomacy intervenes
But it is a standard military inclination
to draw a veil of misinformation

on strikes planned against a target nation

to blow its defences to smithereens

So let us hope that before too long
there will be an evolution
in human mentality
although it would be remarkable to see
an aggressor repent
to avoid a global fatality

But it is only a callow fancy of mine
In my life I've yet to see some sign
that the words once uttered by Einstein

"Two things are certain: The stupidity of the human
race and the infinity of the universe. The latter
has yet to be proven."

have ever been taken note of

WHERE THERE'S A WILL THERE'S A WAY
Where there's a will there's a way
My father used to say
But he could never envision
A world so fast
It could take your breath away
The early bird may catch the worm
But you can never be early enough
Two minutes late
And you've lost your place
Sorry man, that's tough

My dad lived way back when
Life was much slower then
We bought all we needed from the corner store
From two little ageless cavemen
Life was easy and sunny
Work was just a place to earn money
With a beer or two in the local pub
There was loads of time to be funny

Now maybe it's time to look back
Before we get a heart attack
The train we're on seems out of control
And it's running on down the track
Maybe it's time to relearn
Cool down and wait for our turn
Negotiating these rapids
No time to play with the kids
That has to be a cause for concern

We used to take time to cook

Sit down and enjoy a good book
Now you're never alone with your mobile phone
The rest you can overlook
Fast food fast cars fast friends
The list just never ends It's time to cool down
Take a look around
And try to comprehend

It's not such a difficult quest
Slow down and keep the best
When we're all agreed
On what we need
We can throw away the rest
Where there's a will there's a way
That's just as true today
When the world slows down
Like paradise refound
It'll be a beautiful place to stay

CONFUSION

Among all this confusion
You may have the illusion
Someone, somewhere is standing by your side
The future is protected
The course of life directed
You just have to relax and take the ride

There are places on this earth
Where the beauty of a birth, is lost
because the starving child may die
While in this democratic nation
This land of education
Food is dumped to keep the prices high

We embrace nice new inventions
With the most trifling of intentions
Playthings, selfies are amusing
It keeps the people passive
As the need becomes more massive
To aid a world we're constantly abusing

Skin deep democracy
Is fuelled by hypocrisy
Empty words, just to secure your vote
After winning an election
There is rarely a new direction
Just relief they've kept the party's ship afloat

If the truth, just once, be told
Political hearts are shrewd and cold
Governing is a well rewarded occupation
Power is seductive
dissenting voters obstructive
Bold but empty words make a submissive nation

SOLITUDE

When solitude surrounds you
Often visions fill your mind
But never if you look for them
In the normal course of time

Of how this world was, long ago
And will be, once again
Before and after history
and the pandemic of men

When solitude envelops you
And your thoughts are running free
to the beauty that has blessed this world
that we are too blind to see

My friend, do you know solitude
with ten billion of us here?
Each of us adding to the pain
Of an ailing biosphere
Solitude is not loneliness
It will lead to inner peace
Your inner eye can see the truth
Your thoughts will find release

Men are afraid of solitude
They seek the madding crowd
Afraid to face the truths they see
When silence is too loud

When solitude envelops you
Take time, and seek the truth
of the paradise put in our hands
In the beauty of earth's youth

YELLER MOON

There's cold yeller moon in a stygian Sky
No stars to give perspective
Shedding ghastly light on a deadened land
Dim, cold, ineffective
It freezes your hope as you stumble on
But it burns inside your head
Urging you still to climb one more hill
To join the grateful dead

The man in the moon looked down on this scene
He sensed there was something wrong
Something was disturbing the geographical gangrene
Something just didn't belong
Then his mouth spread wide in a mirthless grin
When he spotted you so near to death
He thought "I'll have some fun with that son of a gun
Before he draws his final breath

"Hey you" he yelled from the sombre void
''I can see you ain't got much time left
I could show you where the water is
but to drink would be considered theft
We don't hold with thieves so nobody grieves
When we sit and watch them die
You'll get a dirt-filled tomb for your final doom
So let me bid you a final goodbye"
"And who are you to decide?" you asked
"What should die and what should be
Your evil power is in it's final hour
And your people will be once again free
Your prisoners are about to resume their rights
To chart their destiny
And the sun is about to shine its light
And your death will be the key"

The evil moon, he heard these words
And his face began to fade
And the sun was reborn in a heaven shorn
of hatred, fear and shade
The people gathered and raised their eyes
To the healing, cleansing rain
Which purified and made them strong
To break shackles, fears and chains

CROSSING THROUGH THE LIVES

Crossing through the lives
of new and brief acquaintances
and they through mine
releases a kaleidoscope of all
the colours of the rainbow

Loves and hates - rights and wrongs
opinions and beliefs
stubbornly clung to

Unchangeable

Some of the more vivid and memorable ones
have caused me to change my preferred direction
and travel with them

for a while

ON THE TRAIN

You served me coffee
with a beautiful smile
and your smile didn't waver
when I gave you the
exact change
No more, no less

Unusually enough
You weren't expecting a tip
and your smile was true
You were enjoying your role in life
which was to give satisfaction
which in turn
gave you satisfaction

TO LOVE, TO BE LOVED, AND TO LIVE

Eleven days left of September
And it's cold for the time of the year
The chill quiet nights that I live in remember
too much, too loud and too clear
I thought about writing a letter

But it lost it's direction in rhyme
Now I feel like those people we pitied before
in a far distant moment in time
I remember a child in the city
Where he pursued his dreams to the fill
And now I can smile and say "hey, what a pity
he didn't learn more of that skill"

Eleven days left of September
In a pain that I cannot forgive
All that's left is the flickering ember
Of the vaguest desire
Of the warmth, of the fire
To love, to be loved, and to live

Eleven days left of September
And the TV's got nothing to say
There's a robot reciting from edited writing
The history man made today
The relentless and cheerful illusion
Which everyone knows is a lie

Mistrust overseeing the displaced who are fleeing
And pay for the honour to die
Why should I bother to listen
To preserve a mad moment in time?
Should I lie on my bed, write fictitious love songs
Using words with innocuous rhyme

Eleven days left of September
And no-one to stand up and say
''Is there no-one here who can remember?
We've got a new war, so let's open the door

All heroes must die anyway"
And if I agree to gaze elsewhere
While you secretly freshen your smile
And if my reaction should give satisfaction
Would I get a good mark in my file
But what if your smile turns to laughter
And the mask that you wear disappears
Would you turn your attention to a Nazi convention

And spit out my name like a sneer
Dark voices created this fortress
This intangible hate barricade
Are they still unaware that the storerooms are bare
And the soldiers must somehow be paid

Eleven days left of September
And the season has no cheer to give
My thoughts long for the flickering ember
Of the vaguest desire
Of the warmth, of the fire
To love, to be loved, and to live

I remember the child in the city
And somehow he reminds me of me
I tried so hard to find him again,
But I failed
My eyes too disillusioned to see

I DON'T KNOW WHAT YOU'RE DOING HERE AT ALL

If you think that you're eyes and your soul
are washed clean by the rain
And you think those are pure thoughts you feel
running round in your brain
You've surrounded and filled with apathy
but still you can ignore the pain
Your chance to make change is long gone
  but you ignore the stain

Then I don't know what you're doing here at al l

Are your sons and your daughters
expected to live in a way
that accepts how things have to be
but themselves they have nothing to say
And a million die in a land that seems
far far away
And you say you're concerned
but you can't change it anyway

Then I don't know what you're doing here at all

And you suppose that they've found the solution
for getting things right
but you still fear to walk through the streets
of your city at night
And the friends that you have are just those
who may bark but not bite
You see homeless asleep in shop doorways
but ignore their plight

Then I don't know what you're doing here at all

REFUGEE

The open barge, filled to the gunnels with faces black and brown unsmiling serious faces devoid of conversation
White eyes searching the horizon for sight of anything except ocean heads and bodies undulating up and down, port and starboard with the heavy unceasing swell of the sea
Silent children held tightly to mamas breast foodless, waterless, with meagre belongings in plastic bags, al l savings given to finance this expensive voyage

All eyes searching the horizon
And then, suddenly, distantly, land Europe!
A chance of life, a future for the kids, freedom from oppression
A collective sigh of relief is followed by a prayer of thanks to their respective gods, not least beacuse the barge is rotten and is perceptibly slowly disintegrating
The coastguard power boat approaches and pulls alongise hesitant words are exchanged a rope is thrown, made fast and they are towed

not towards Europe, but towards Africa Europe subsides beneath the hori zon they are released from the towing rope The coastguard roars away
The wreckage of the barge is found the next day
There is no sign of survivors

THE CHANGING OF THE WAYS

The old man didn't know me when I saw him on the street But I
knew him for my father, vaguely studying his feet I stumbled closer
to him, and took his withered hand and though he finally found
my face, he didn't understand
We became surrounded by shoppers, their eyes alight with fear
How can you reignite the past when the future is so clear I told
them I reject you all , I choose my father instead some woman
screamed hysterically you know he should be dead And who are
you to say I said what should die and what should be

Have. you got the kind of eyes that see so much more than me
Let the past be resurrected, there is nothing to be burned
There are honours to be given there are lessons to be learned
How could you have forgotten the truths of long ago
That now are myths growing rotten with the weight of all we think
we know I won't stop you living for tomorrow you can build castles
in the air
Then you'll have to steal or borrow a past to know that you are
there
The age of superstition has almost passed us by
Gone are inhibitions, those tears are almost dry
So now we face a future with no traditions of the past
And as I turned away from them they stared at me aghast
I took my father by the hand and led him through the throng
I brought him to a place I know where eternity lives in song
Judging present, judging future by what has gone before
For what we were is what we are - the truth, not less or more

FAGS - (Slang for cigarette in the UK)

If you ask for a fag in the USA
Provocation
While in Blighty you just get a smoke In the States it's supposed deviation Thou some might laugh - it's a joke
Don't try to ask for a packet of fags
"The blow up kind?" they might inquire
It strikes you that you've made a cock up
And that, you might be the object of desire
Not that it matters too much, these days
Desegregation
It's in that they're all coming out
Seen hand in hand in some parts of the land
Simply just strolling about
Good luck to all , that's all I can say
Ifi relieved we got rid of that stress
And if I think back, for a good many years
Society couldn't care less

GLEN HAVALEEK SINGLE MALT

We opened up another bottle of whisky
The situation just as clear as mud
My thoughts told me "these guys are much too risky and another bottle of scotch won't do no good" I'd met them in a bar in downtown Philly

And Yd said my name was J. of Nazareth
I looked the part and they all seemed to believe me
Though they sure could smell the whisky on my breath

So we ended up in this one room apartment With another bottle of whisky going down fast And Tom said "Jesus, see this bottle? This bottle , Jesus buddy, is the last

And Jesus, as this bottle now is empty I'll just fill it up with water at the sink and a miracle you'll make, just like you used to And make that water something fit to drink"

He placed the refilled bottle on the table
And a shadow of my fate passed before my eyes
I said that I was somewhat out of practice
"But I'll do the best I can, just trust me guys
You'll have to leave the room for just ten minutes
While I have a little conversation with my pa
When it comes to holy spells to produce whisky
He and Gabriel have the biggest repertoire"

None of them good ole boys was ever doubtful and I figured none of them could ever afford to miss the chance to try even a mouthful of some holy spirit distilled by the lord When they left I poured the water down the sink and filled it up again - no trouble at all The colour looked real good, good enough to drink a little bit of foam, but the bubbles were quite small
When they came back the bottle was full to overfl owing

And they regarded it with a kind of religious awe

But I'd figured out which way the wind was blowing
But the boys still stood between me and the door ‖ Boys" , I said, "this stuff ain't from Kentucky and we have to give it a little piece of respect my pa was in a good mood and we got lucky now I'm bound to do what my pa would surely expect
I've got to offer thanks for this here manna before pa gets sore and maybe changes his mind

I gotta abase myself under the night sky's heavenly banner
Pa don't often give perks to humankind
Well, them boys moved aside with alacrity
"Sure Jesus, a man's gotta do what he's gotta do ‖ I placed my palms together with holy dignity
Walked through them to the door and went on through

GLEN HAVALEEK II

Running down them stairs was just like flying
Then I took off with some tempo down the road
I reckoned speed was a better choice than dying
Just like Jesus, but without his heavy load
I never forgot that evening and that meeting
but I never expected to meet with a time bomb
A year later a voice hailed me in greeting
I turned round and turned pale, it was Tom

"Well Jesus buddy, it's sure been quite a while
and to see you here, well , that's a nice surprise
I sure did my best to force a nervous smile
to hide the trepidation in my eyes
It's a pity that you had to leave us buddy
But I know that you had your pa to thank
Well, we drank his scotch and it was goody goody
That was the finest bottle of scotch we'd ever drank

Well we parted after we'd sat down and had a beer
Me with a talent I never knew I had
It sure was strange to sit with Tom and hear
about the talent which I didn't get from my dad
It's nice to be a walking distillery
with a continuous production, so to speak
With a multipurpose swinging attached artillery
For that rarest of single malts, Glen Havaleek

Printed in Poland
by Amazon Fulfillment
Poland Sp. z o.o., Wrocław
04 June 2022

0f20b90f-d727-4556-8b20-4ebd19b19807R01